AF583888

TIWI WAR KWAMPINI

TIWI WAR HERO

Nyirratuwu Ruth Pakiliyanuwu

For Ruth

About the Indigenous Literacy Foundation

The Indigenous Literacy Foundation (ILF) is a national charity working with Aboriginal and Torres Strait Islander remote Communities across Australia. We are Community-led, responding to requests from remote Communities for culturally relevant books, including early learning board books, resources, and programs to support Communities to create and publish their stories in languages of their choice.

In 2024 the ILF won the Astrid Lindgren Memorial Award, given annually to a person or organisation for their outstanding contribution to children's or young adult literature.

First published in 2026 by the Indigenous Literacy Foundation

Gadigal Country

Level 17/207 Kent Street
Sydney NSW 2000
ilf.org.au

Cataloguing-in-Publication details are available from the National Library of Australia
www.trove.nla.gov.au

ISBN 9781922592712

Typesetting and design by Holly Doran, Indigenous Literacy Foundation
Printed in China by RR Donnelley Asia Printing Solutions Limited

Written, translated and illustrated by Mavis Kerinaiua
with support from Laura Rademaker

Nginanki Tiwi history ngini Second World War purruwurtiyarra Louie'ngarra-ngirimipi. Ningani wuta Tiwi nimarra wurimi nanki awarra ngirramini.

Wuta paparliwi purrumwari nanki mwarlapwara ngini ngapapuruka wutawa ngirramini ngini putuwurupura.

This is the Tiwi history of the Second World War as told by Louie's family. Tiwi people still talk about this story today.

Our ancestors left footprints for us to follow their ways.

Ngiya-amini Louie Purraputimali ngarra ngarra pupuni. Ngarra yiminga Yarinapilini clan (red ochre). Ngarra japuja yima kapi mission tingata wuta kiringarra ngarra-mamirampi.

My grandfather Louie Purraputimali was a strong family man. He was of the Yarinapilini clan (red ochre). He lived on the beach at Nguiu Mission with his six children.

Tayikwapi Tiwi wupamurrumi kapi Black Watch karri Second World War. Wuta wurumamula Black Diggers.

Wuta tangarima pirimani kapi warta yinkitayi Tarntipi tingata awungarruwu kapi Makapurumuwu amintiya kiyi pakinya kurlala, pirripangulimayi tingatangala.

Awuta army pirikirimi yangamini ningani mwarliki-yanga ngarimamula Marralangampi.

Many Tiwi served in the Black Watch during the Second World War. They were known as the Black Diggers.

They would camp out in the bush near Tarntipi Beach at a place called Makapurumuwu and begin their patrol along the beaches.

The army dug a water hole now called Marralangampi.

Awinyirra American DC-3 wurra yipila yirrima jiyimi kapi Nguiu Mission airstrip. Louie amintiya ngarra-mirani Kuwalinga (Harry Munkara) puruwani awuta pilots, amintiya Tiwi arikutumunuwi purruwunga awinyirra parts. Anapanara awuta kurrajakayuwi wuta wiyi wunipakupawurli.

An American DC-3 plane had made an emergency landing at the mission airstrip. Louie and his son Harry Munkara helped the pilots, and Tiwi people eventually salvaged the parts. After that, the mission became a target for the Japanese. Soon the Japanese would be back.

627

Waya karri japinari 19 February 1942 ngarra Louie yipakurluwuni awuta wurra yirrima kapi yuwuka waya kuriyuwu-nara kangi Nguiu.

It was early in the morning on 19 February 1942 when Louie saw Japanese planes flying over Nguiu.

Ninkiyi, yingwapa wurra purruwuriyi palanganya-wani amintiya aripa-wani kiyi turli pirimi Nguiu Mission. Ngini jurra piripirni!

Ngarra piraya yimpanga, yimi, yati tini turli pirimi kangi ngarra yirrikarla. Waya ngini karrikuwapi Tiwi turli pirimi.

Suddenly, some of the planes broke formation and gunned the mission. The church was hit!

Luckily, there was only one casualty, but it could have been much, much worse.

Louie kalikali yimi kapi Father McGrath pili yuwurtimati ngini yinuwaya-ngirri Jiliyati ngini Japanese waya wunuwuja, api awuta arikurtumunuwi kapi Jiliyati karluwu kuwa pirimi ngirramini kangi radio kapi Nguiu Mission.

Louie ran to Father McGrath so he could warn Darwin the Japanese were coming, but the people in Darwin did not listen to the message on the radio from Nguiu Mission.

Ninkiyi ngarra Louie yinimarruriyi awuta Tiwi yilaruwu kapi paparinga awungaji kapi Gabriel Gardens pirimiringarra awungaji. Kiyi warta pirikirimi mintawunga amintiya purruwunga yinkiti ngini purruwapa.

Meanwhile, Louie led the Tiwi people to the mangroves at Gabriel Gardens to hide. He built shelters and hunted food for the families.

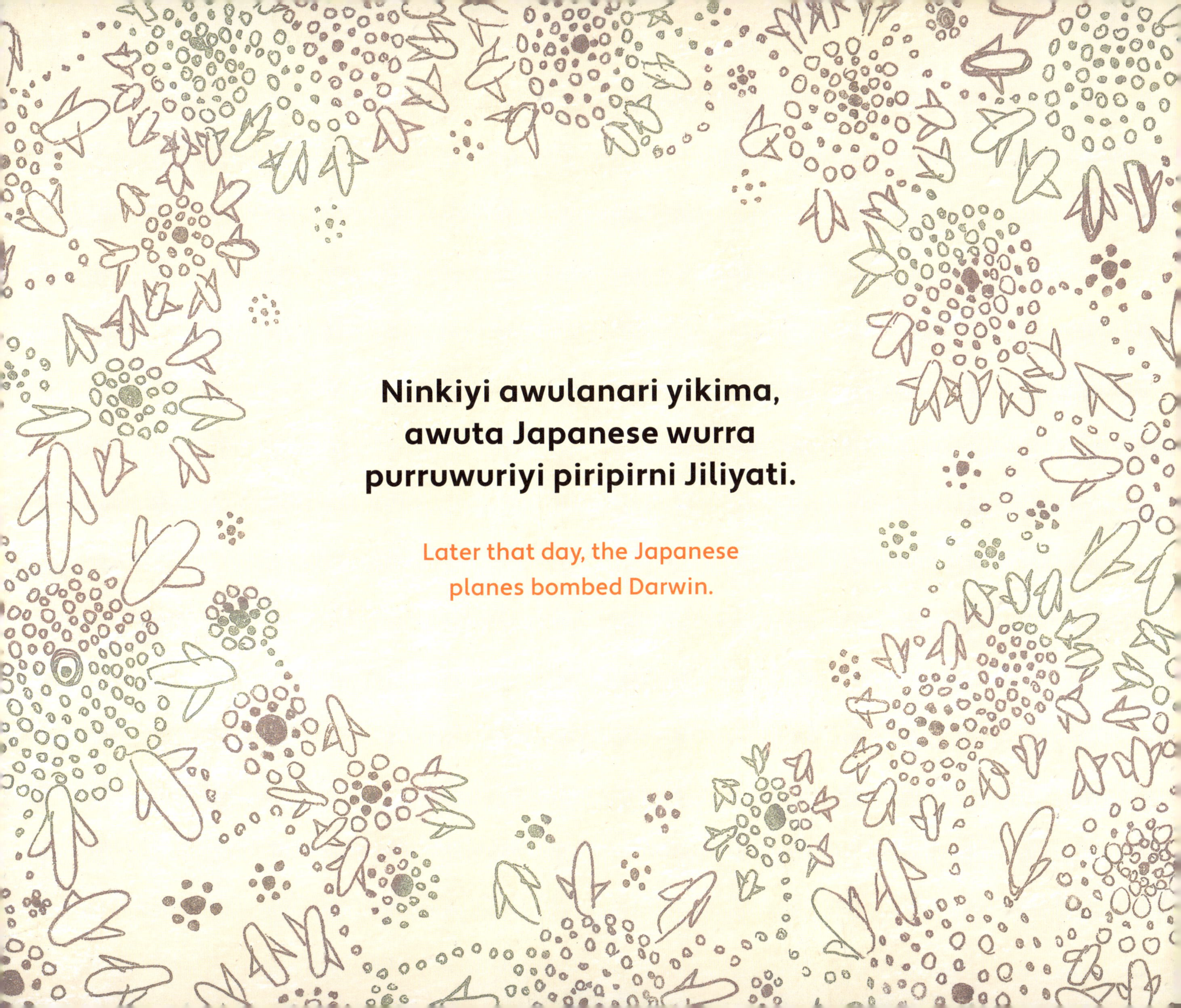

Ninkiyi awulanari yikima, awuta Japanese wurra purruwuriyi piripirni Jiliyati.

Later that day, the Japanese planes bombed Darwin.

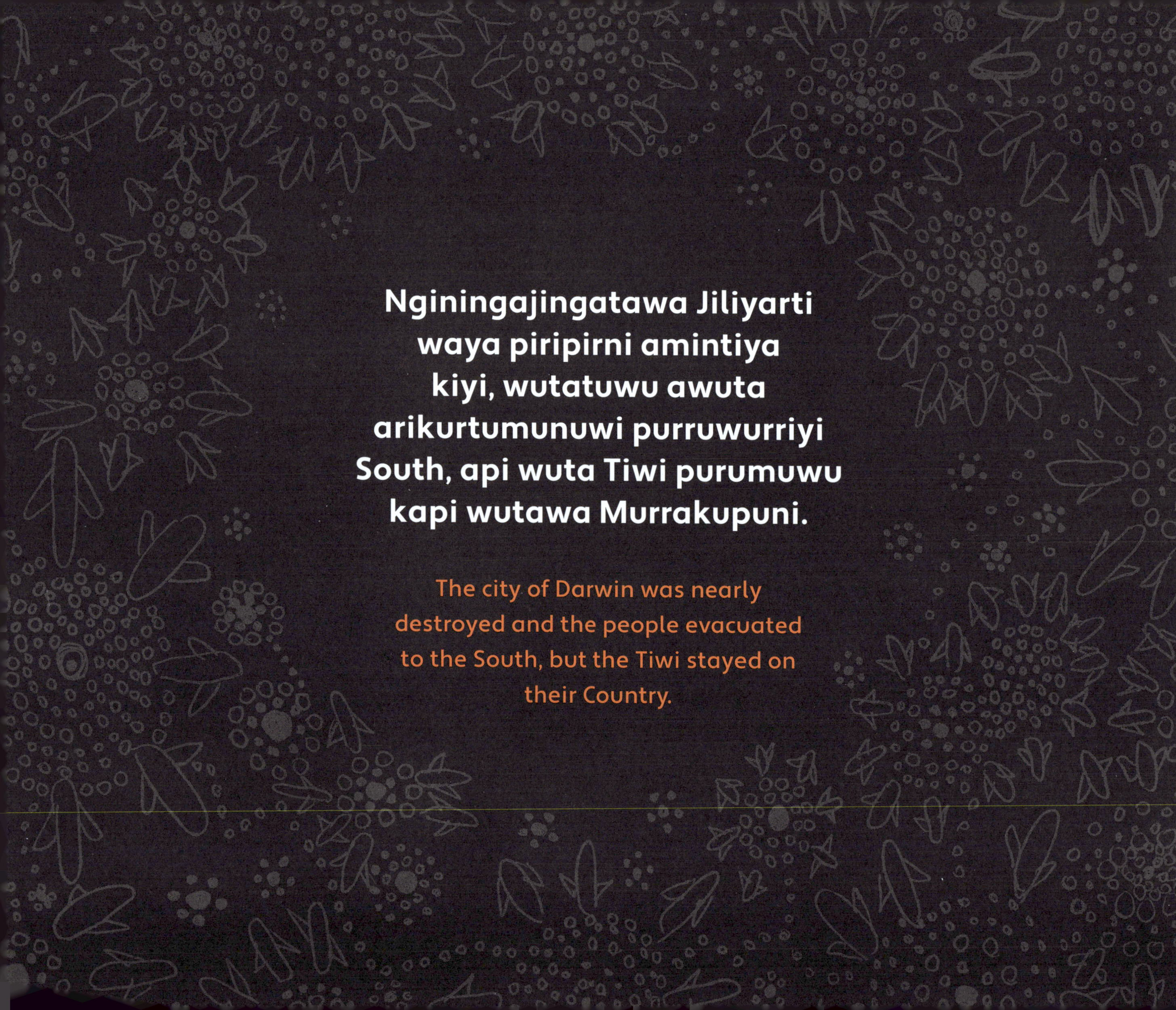

Ngininingajingatawa Jiliyarti waya piripirni amintiya kiyi, wutatuwu awuta arikurtumunuwi purruwurriyi South, api wuta Tiwi purumuwu kapi wutawa Murrakupuni.

The city of Darwin was nearly destroyed and the people evacuated to the South, but the Tiwi stayed on their Country.

Jikilarruwu kapi Wurrumiyanga ratuwati ngini wuta purumuwu awungaji Wilipingirraga. Api ngarra Louie kurlala yimamani awungaji live mines kapi winga, kiyi, ngarra yipakurluwuni awinyirra *Don Isidro* kapala nyirra tumpunari. Kiyi jipingarti.

Cape Fourcroy on Bathurst Island was their lookout. As Louie patrolled there looking for live mines in the water, he saw a ship, *Don Isidro*, in trouble. It had been hit!

Yirrima yimi! Kiyi, yikirimi yikwani pili yimatamangi awinyirra maratinga kapi warta. Api karluwu, nyirra *Don Isidro* waya yipingarti. Wutatuwu awuta crew purrupumwari awinyirra maratinga.

Quick! He made a fire to guide the ship to safety, but it was too late. *Don Isidro* was sinking. The crew abandoned ship.

Karri yinkitayi jipingarti awinyirra maratinga, api ngarra Louie mwaliki yimi amintiya yuwunga awuta yuwurrara crewmen api awungarri waya Don Isidro jimajingupura karrampi kapi Cape Fourcroy Jikilarruwu.

Ngini mission lugger, St. Francis, amintiya HMAS Warrnambool purruwuriyi kurlalaga pirimani awuta survivors.

Before it was too late, Louie swam out and rescued two crewmen as Don Isidro drifted towards Cape Fourcroy.

The mission lugger, St. Francis, and HMAS Warrnambool searched for survivors.

Awinyirra mission's lugger jurrumumi jiyimi yikwani. Ngarra Louie mwarliki yimi tuwawanga, yuwunga awuta yurrajirrima kiyi, yinimarruriyi warta, pirripakupawurli mission.

Karri wuta purruwunga yinkiti (supplies) kangi *Don Isidro* awuta Tiwi putuwunga yingarti yinkiti ngini purruwapa amintiya kukunari pirimi ngini ngininga jingatawa wumunga.

The mission lugger caught fire. Louie swam out again and rescued three people, bringing them to safety at the mission.

When they opened the supplies from the wreck of *Don Isidro* the Tiwi had enough food to feast on for weeks on end!

SF.

Nyonga wumunga ngarra yuwurtiyarra awuta Tiwi alalinguwi ngini wuta kurlalaga mwalapwara jarrumwani kangi tingata ngini ngamatakupawurlamigi awuta survivors kapi warta.

Wuta purruwunayi mwarlapwara! Api awarra mwarlapwara angi-wutawa lucky survivors.

Api awuta crew kangi *Don Isidro* karluwu yimpanga pirimi. Yingawpa pirripamurlujupa yiloti kapi winga.

Tiwi ngirimpi pirayi pirimi amintiya pirikijika awarra captain awungarruwu yinkitayi kangi jupunyini awungaji kapi Pawunampi, pirripakupawurli angitawa coat kapi mission.

The next morning, he told the Tiwi boys to look for any footprints on the beach so they could bring any survivors to safety.

They found some prints! The footprints led them to the lucky survivors.

But many of the crew of *Don Isidro* did not survive. Some were lost at sea.

Tiwi family said a prayer and buried the captain in the dunes at Cape Fourcroy, returning his coat to the mission.

Api ninganuwanga war, ngarra yuwuriyi yipamurrumi kangi Black Watch awungaji kapi Cape Fourcroy lookout kapi Wiyapurali timani, awngamji ngini wuta kurluwuni kurrujakayuwi wunipila.

Awinyirra kurrujakayi wurra turli pirimi. Awuta pingininginta kurrujakayuwi fighters pirimajungupura kangi winga ngini najingatawa wumunga.

As the war went on, Louie continued his work in the Black Watch from Cape Fourcroy at a place called Wiyapurali, on lookout for another Japanese attack.

A Japanese plane was shot down. The five Japanese fighters floated on the water for days.

Mamana, purruwuriyi karri pirrapirtingaya awarra pujinga. Api pirripakuluwunyi pinginingita kurrujakayuwi soldiers pirimajunguriyi kangi awarra rubber dinghy. Wuta kunyani nginingaji wuta allies, api ngarra Louie yipakurluwunyi Japanese badges kapi wuta kuluji. Api kuriyuwu yikirimani ngatawa walamani kiyi yuwunga awuta.

Louie yumwariyi ngarra-mamirampi ngini wupamangi awuta soldiers kiyi, yuwuriyi yipakupawurli kapi mission pili yuwutimarti yangatuwuni.

Wuta pirimarruriyi awuta kurrujakayuwi soldiers kapi mission amintiya mwarliki pirimi kurrakala kangi Apsley Strait.

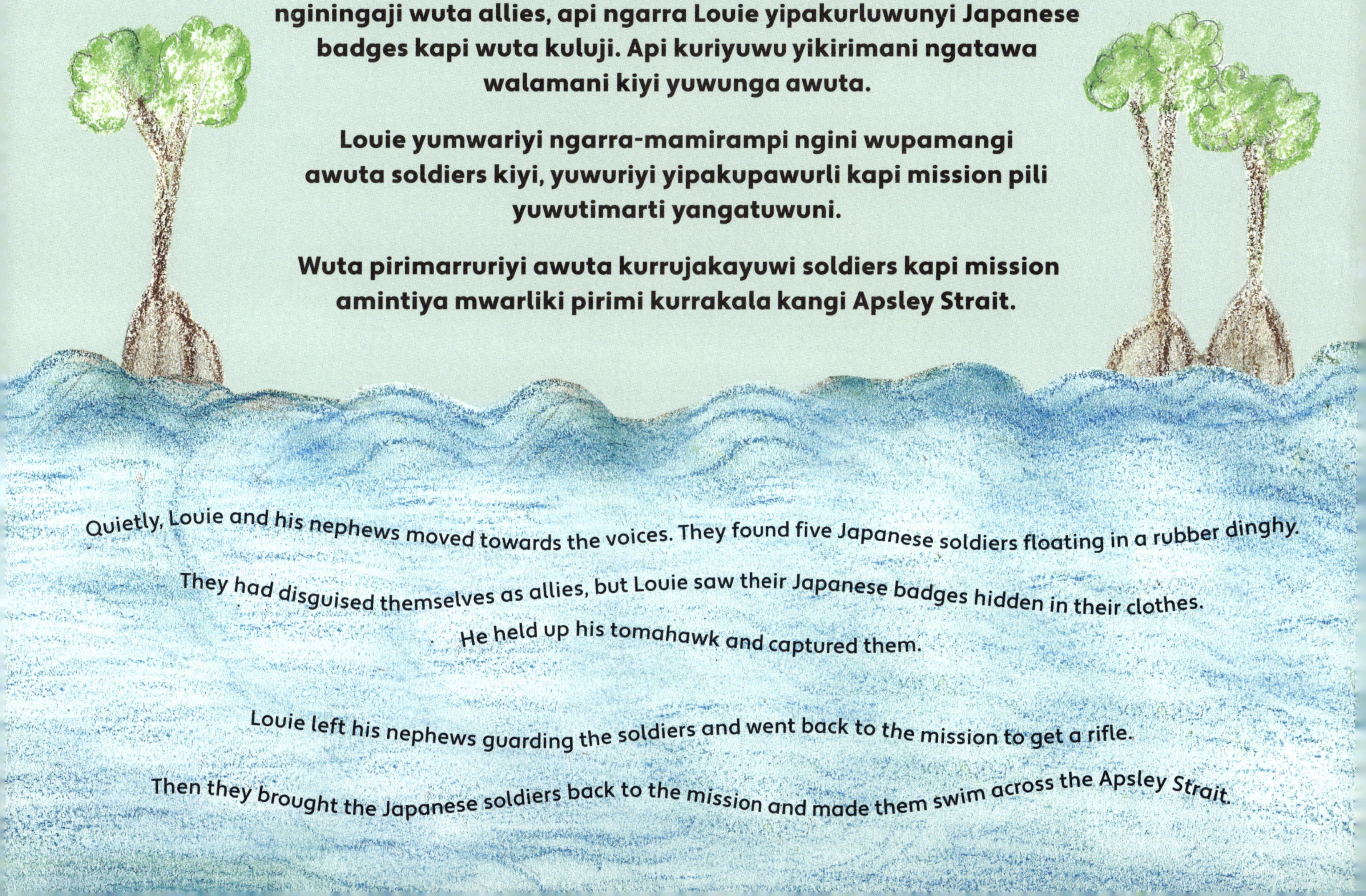

Quietly, Louie and his nephews moved towards the voices. They found five Japanese soldiers floating in a rubber dinghy.

They had disguised themselves as allies, but Louie saw their Japanese badges hidden in their clothes.

He held up his tomahawk and captured them.

Louie left his nephews guarding the soldiers and went back to the mission to get a rifle.

Then they brought the Japanese soldiers back to the mission and made them swim across the Apsley Strait.

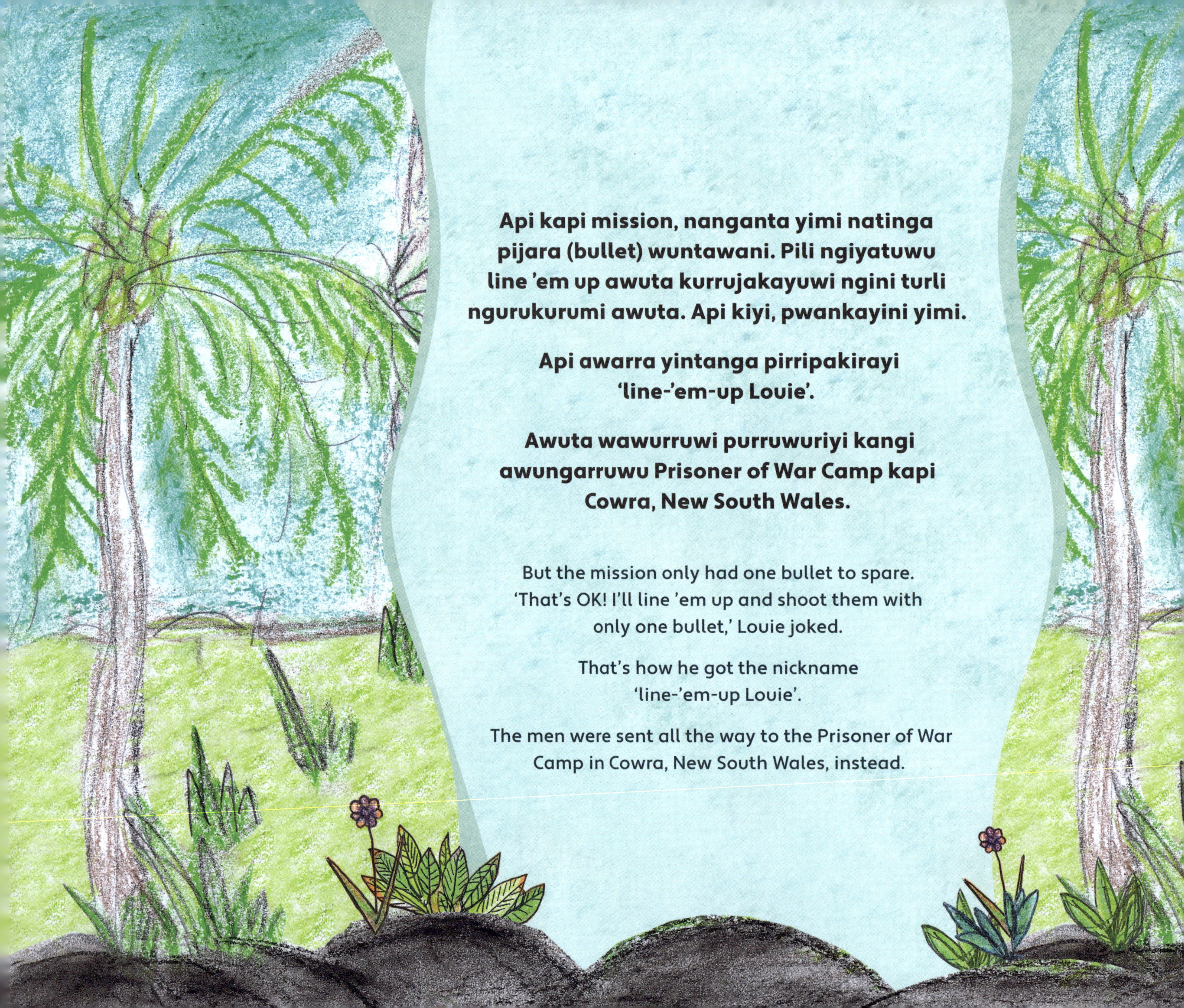

Api kapi mission, nanganta yimi natinga pijara (bullet) wuntawani. Pili ngiyatuwu line 'em up awuta kurrujakayuwi ngini turli ngurukurumi awuta. Api kiyi, pwankayini yimi.

Api awarra yintanga pirripakirayi 'line-'em-up Louie'.

Awuta wawurruwi purruwuriyi kangi awungarruwu Prisoner of War Camp kapi Cowra, New South Wales.

But the mission only had one bullet to spare. 'That's OK! I'll line 'em up and shoot them with only one bullet,' Louie joked.

That's how he got the nickname 'line-'em-up Louie'.

The men were sent all the way to the Prisoner of War Camp in Cowra, New South Wales, instead.

Ngarra ngiya-amini ngarra ngawa warntarrana kwapini.

Ngawa ngintimatangiliparra nuwa, ngini putuputuwu nguntakirayi nuwa kapi waya pirranyumi pirimi, kapi Second World War. May they rest in eternal peace.

Ngawurraningurumangi awuta kapi pirranyumi amintiya awuta kapi wurumuru ningani kapi war.

Lest we forget.

Pongki to all.

Mana nimpangi.

My aminayi (grandfather) is my champion, my unsung kwapini (hero).

We acknowledge and pay our deepest respects to the Tiwi and those of all nations who lost loved ones in the Second World War. May they rest in eternal peace.

We remember all who lost their lives, those who served and those whose lives were changed by war.

Lest we forget

Peace to all.

Farewell.

Timor Sea
Dundas Strait
TIWI ISLANDS
Clarence Strait
Apsley Strait
Yirrfiti Island
Pangtina Is. (Vernon Is.)
Tree point
Arafura Sea
Beagle Gulf

Photo by John Brown, Justin O'Brien Collection

Wurikirimi

Nginaki pupuni ngirramini ngini awarra nanki project ngapamurrumi ngininaki jurra amintiya ngini tayikuwapi puranji awarra nanki ngirramini ngini history.

Ngawa kukunari ngini service of Australian armed forces amintiya Missionaries of the Scared Heart ngini wuta warntirrana awarra nanki ngirramini.

Ngawa kukunari kapi awuta Tiwi Community amintiya Indigenous Literacy Foundation ngini awarra nanki pirikirimi nginanki jurra warntirrana, Fiona Kerinaiua, Ancilla Kurrupuwu amimtiya Jacinta Alimankinni.

Kapi ngawa-amini Louis Purraputimali Munkara amintiya ngiya-naringa Ruth Pakiliyanuwu Kerinaiua amintiya awuta Munkara amintiya yingwapa ngirimipi, Ngiya arnukwa ngintimatangiliparra nuwa. Nuwa nguri.

Ngawa karluwu ngintimatangiliparra nuwa ngawa-amini amintiya Jikilawula family, amintiya ngarra kakirijuwi ngarra-mamirampi: Thecla, Odilla, Harold, Beatrice Kerinaiua (nee Munkara); amintiya wuta yuwuni Harry.

Nginanki project wuta Australian National University wuntawani 'Beyond Reconciliation: Truth-Telling for Indigenous Wellbeing' amintiya Australian Research Council (grant no. DE220100042).

Nuwa nguri.

Mavis Kerinaiua

It is a special privilege being part of this project and it has been an honour making this book and illustrations for everyone to learn and enjoy history.

We acknowledge the service of the Australian armed forces and the Missionaries of the Sacred Heart for their bravery.

We thank the whole Tiwi Community and the Indigenous Literacy Foundation for making this book a reality, especially Fiona Kerinaiua, Ancilla Kurrupuwu and Jacinta Alimankinni.

To my grandfather Louis Purraputimali Munkara and my dearest mother Ruth Pakiliyanuwu Kerinaiua and the Munkara and other extended family, I give my deepest thanks.

I also wish to acknowledge my late grandfather's family, the Jikilawula family, and his late children: Thecla; Odilla; Harold; Beatrice Kerinaiua (née Munkara); and their brother Harry.

This project was supported by the Australian National University's project 'Beyond Reconciliation: Truth-Telling for Indigenous Wellbeing' and the Australian Research Council (grant no. DE220100042).

Thank you.

Mavis Kerinaiua